S0-CEY-203

JAVIER COVO TORRES

THE MAYAS
ON THE ROCKS

Dante

THE MAYAS ON THE ROCKS

1st edition: Editorial Dante. 2007
ISBN: 970-605-377-8

Cover: Javier Covo Torres
Illustration: Javier Covo Torres
Translation: David phillips
Copy checking: Laura Morales

All rights reserved
© Javier Covo Torres
©Editorial Dante S.A. de C.V.
Calle 19 No. 102 x 20 Colonia México. C.P. 97125
Mérida, Yucatán, México

Complete or partial reproduction of this book by any printed, digital
or electronic means is strictly prohibited.

PRINTED IN CHINA

THE MAYAS
ON THE ROCKS

BY

Covo

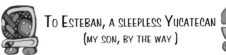 To Esteban, a sleepless Yucatecan
(my son, by the way)

CONTENT

THE ORIGIN OF THE MAYAS

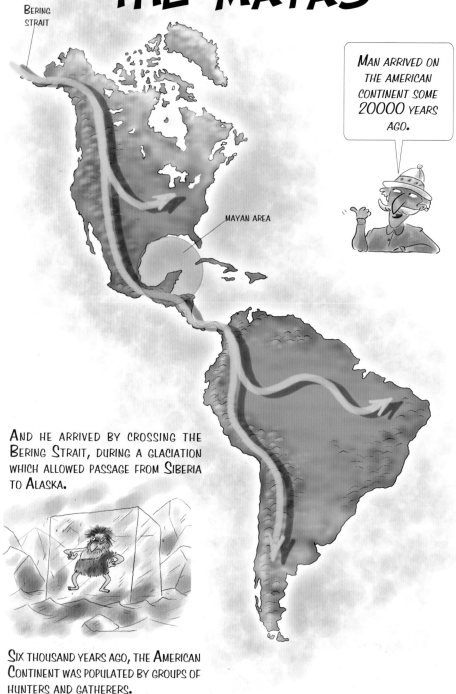

BERING STRAIT

MAYAN AREA

MAN ARRIVED ON THE AMERICAN CONTINENT SOME *20000* YEARS AGO.

AND HE ARRIVED BY CROSSING THE BERING STRAIT, DURING A GLACIATION WHICH ALLOWED PASSAGE FROM SIBERIA TO ALASKA.

SIX THOUSAND YEARS AGO, THE AMERICAN CONTINENT WAS POPULATED BY GROUPS OF HUNTERS AND GATHERERS.

IN THE YEAR 2000 BEFORE OUR ERA, ALL OF THE MESOAMERICAN REGION WAS SETTLED.

SUN FOR SALE

BETWEEN THE YEARS 3000 AND 2000,

WE WERE ALREADY HERE.

IN THE YEAR 1000 BEFORE OUR ERA, AGRICULTURE HAD ALREADY DEVELOPED,

AND THE TOWNS OF MESOAMERICA HAD A UNIFORM CULTURE.

THE LAND OF THE MAYAS

The ancient Maya lived in a territory covering 400,000 square kilometers which includes several states of Mexico, the republics of Guatemala and Belize, and parts of Honduras and El Salvador.

> To make things clearer, we are going to divide the Mayan area into three zones: the North Zone, the Central Zone, and the South Zone.

Campeche

Tabasco

MEXICO

GUATEMALA

EL SALV

SOUTH ZONE

This includes the Pacific Coast, the Guatemalan Mountains, a zone of El Salvador, and part of the Mexican state of Chiapas. It has active volcanoes and the Usumacinta and Motagua rivers are born in its mountains.

The first social organization among the Maya arose on the Pacific coast.

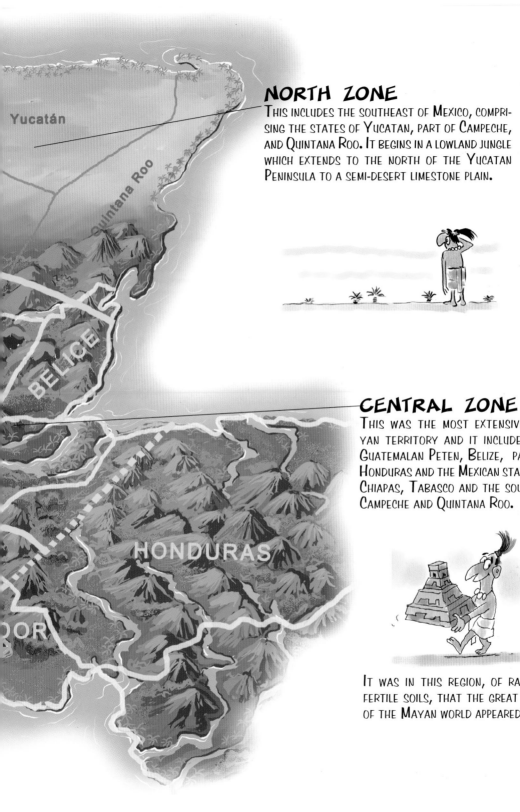

Yucatán

Quintana Roo

BELICE

HONDURAS

DOR

NORTH ZONE

This includes the southeast of Mexico, comprising the states of Yucatan, part of Campeche, and Quintana Roo. It begins in a lowland jungle which extends to the north of the Yucatan Peninsula to a semi-desert limestone plain.

CENTRAL ZONE

This was the most extensive Mayan territory and it included the Guatemalan Peten, Belize, part of Honduras and the Mexican states of Chiapas, Tabasco and the south of Campeche and Quintana Roo.

It was in this region, of rain and fertile soils, that the great towns of the Mayan world appeared.

HISTORICAL PERIODS

THE MAYAN HISTORICAL ERAS ARE:

- **PRECLASSIC PERIOD**

- **CLASSIC PERIOD**
  THE MAYAN COLLAPSE

- **POSTCLASSIC PERIOD**

PRECLASSIC PERIOD
(1500 B.C - 150 A.D.)

- **EARLY PRECLASSIC**
  (1500 B.C. - 800 B.C.)
- **MIDDLE PRECLASSIC**
  (800 B.C. - 300 B.C.)
- **LATE PRECLASSIC**
  (300 B.C. - 150 A.D.)

CLASSIC PERIOD
(150 A.D - 900 A.D.)

- **PROTOCLASSIC**
  (150 A.D. - 300 A.D.)
- **EARLY CLASSIC**
  (300 A.D. - 600 A.D.)
- **LATE CLASSIC**
  (600 A.D. - 900 A.D.)

THE MAYAN COLLAPSE

POSTCLASSIC PERIOD
(1000 A.D. - 1541 A.D.)

- **EARLY POSTCLASSIC**
  (1000 A.D. - 1250 A.D.)
- **LATE POSTCLASSIC**
  (1250 A.D. - 1541 A.D.)

PRECLASSIC PERIOD

EARLY PRECLASSIC
(1500 B.C. - 800 B.C.)

> IT'S SIMPLE: WE SOW AND THEN WE PUT OURSELVES IN THE HANDS OF THE RAIN GOD.

IN THE BEGINNING THE MAYA LIVED IN VILLAGES, THEY GREW MAIZE WHICH THEY NEEDED TO SURVIVE, AND THEY PRACTICED MAGIC TO ENSURE GOOD CROPS.

MIDDLE PRECLASSIC
(800 B.C. - 300 B.C.)

WHEN THERE WAS MAIZE IN ABUNDANCE, SOCIETY BEGAN TO DIVIDE. ONE GROUP DEDICATED ITSELF TO WITCHCRAFT: THEY WERE THE FIRST MAYAN PRIESTS.

THE OLMECS ARRIVED DURING THIS PERIOD, BRINGING WITH THEM THE CALENDAR, WRITING, THE CULT OF THE JAGUAR, AND THE PRACTICE OF SCULPTING LARGE HUMAN HEADS.

NOT FOR NOTHING IS THE OLMEC CULTURE CONSIDERED THE MOTHER OF ALL MEXICAN CULTURES.

LATE PRECLASSIC
(300 B.C. - 150 A.D.)

TOWARDS THE END OF THE PRECLASSIC, THE
MAYA IMPROVED THE CALENDAR, AND INVENTED
THE ZERO AND HIEROGLYPHIC WRITING.

WITH POWER IN THE HANDS OF THE SORCERERS, TWO
TYPES OF MAYA APPEARED: THE ONES THAT CARRIED
THE LOAD AND THE ONES THAT HAD IT CARRIED.

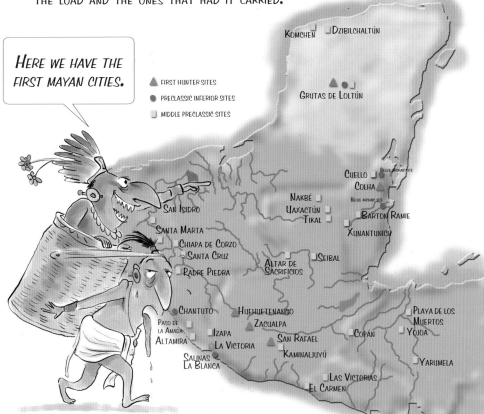

HERE WE HAVE THE
FIRST MAYAN CITIES.

▲ FIRST HUNTER SITES

● PRECLASSIC INFERIOR SITES

▢ MIDDLE PRECLASSIC SITES

KOMCHEN
DZIBILCHALTÚN

GRUTAS DE LOLTÚN

CUELLO
COLHA
BELIZE ARCHAIC SITE

NAKBÉ
UAXACTÚN
TIKAL
BELIZE ARCHAIC SITE
BARTON RAMIE
XUNANTUNICH

SAN ISIDRO

SANTA MARTA
CHIAPA DE CORZO
SANTA CRUZ
PADRE PIEDRA

ALTAR DE
SACRIFICIOS
SEIBAL

CHANTUTO
HUEHUETENANGO
PLAYA DE LOS
MUERTOS
PASO DE
LA AMADA
ZACUALPA
YOJOA
ALTAMIRA
IZAPA
LA VICTORIA
SAN RAFAEL
COPÁN
SALINAS
LA BLANCA
KAMINALJUYÚ
YARUMELA

LAS VICTORIAS
EL CARMEN

CLASSIC PERIOD

It was in the Classic period that the Mayan boom took place: six centuries of splendor when the great kingdoms reached their apogee.

The priests, who controlled the calendar, art and writing, instigated a theocracy based on fear.

PROTOCLASSIC

(150 A.D.- 300 A.D.)

AT THE BEGINNING OF THE CLASSIC PE-
RIOD SOCIAL DIVISIONS ACCENTUATED.

MORE AND BETTER CEREMONIAL CENTERS APPEARED.
IN THE YEAR 300, THE CITIES OF *TIKAL*
AND *COPAN* GREW UNDER THE GOVERN-
MENT OF GREAT DYNASTIES.

◻ PRECLASSIC OR PROTOCLASSIC SITES

● MONUMENTAL SCULPTURE SITES

◻ IZAPAN STYLE

DZIBILCHALTÚN
ACANCEH
CHICHÉN ITZÁ
YAXUNÁ
MANÍ
KABAH
LOLTÚN
HOLACTÚN
SANTA ROSA XTAMPAK

BELLOTE
CALAKMUL
CERROS
SAN MIGUEL
EL MIRADOR
NAKBÉ
LAMANAI
UAXACTÚN
SAN JOSÉ
HOLMUL
BARTON RAMIE
TIKAL
XUNANTUNICH
SAN AGUSTÍN
TZIMINKAX
CHIAPA DE CORZO
SANTA CRUZ
ALTAR DE
SACRIFICIOS
SANTA ROSA
SAN FELIPE
TONALÁ
LA LAGUNITA
SANTA RITA
UTATLÁN
EL PORTÓN
ABAJ
ZACUALPA
IZAPA
TAKALIK CHUCUMUK
COPÁN
EL HOBO
KAMINALJUYÚ
SALINAS—
LA BLANCA
CHOCOLÁ
EL BAÚL
YARUMELA
MONTE ALTO
OBERO
FINCA
ARIZONA
CHALCHUAPA
USULUTÁN

AND WHAT'S
WORSE IS THAT
HE DOESN'T
WANT TO GO ON
A DIET.

EARLY CLASSIC
(300 A.D. - 600 A.D.)

AGRICULTURE PROSPERED WITH THE USE OF TERRACES AND WATERING CHANNELS, COMMERCE EXPANDED BEYOND THE FRONTIERS.

THE GREAT INTELLECTUAL ACCOMPLISHMENTS (ASTRONOMY, THE CALENDARS, WRITING AND MATHEMATICS), BECAME ARMS OF POWER:

THE POPULATION GREW AND THROUGHOUT THE MAYAN WORLD CEREMONIAL CENTERS EMERGED WITH TEMPLES, PYRAMIDS, PALACES AND BALL GAMES.

THE MAYAN CULTURE TOOK OFF!

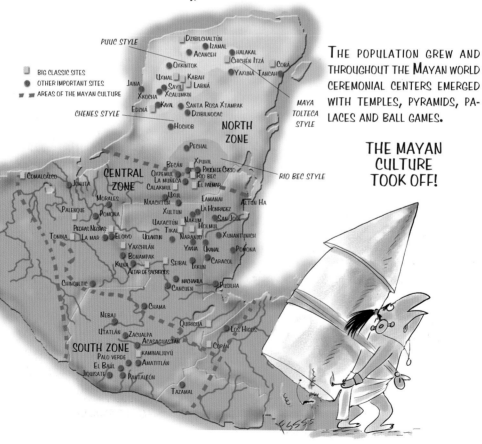

PUUC STYLE

BIG CLASSIC SITES
OTHER IMPORTANT SITES
AREAS OF THE MAYAN CULTURE

CHENES STYLE

DZIBILCHALTÚN
IZAMAL
ACANCEH   HALAKAL
OXKINTOK   CHICHEN ITZÁ
                          YAXUNÁ TANCAH   COBÁ
UXMAL   KABAH
JAINA   SAYIL   LABNÁ
XKOCHA   XCALUMKIN
          KAYAL   SANTA ROSA XTAMPAK   MAYA
EDZNÁ   DZIBILNOCAC   TOLTECA
                                                    STYLE
HOCHOB   NORTH ZONE

PECHAL

                    XPUHIL
          BECÁN   PASIÓN DE CRISTO
COMALCALCO   OXPEMUL   RÍO BEC   RÍO BEC STYLE
          CENTRAL   LA MUÑECA
JONUTA   ZONE   CALAKMUL   EL PALMAR
          UXUL
MORALES   NAACHTÚN   LAMANAI   ALTUN HA
PALENQUE   POMONA   XULTUN   LA HONRADEZ
                    UAXACTÚN   NAKUM   SAN JOSÉ
          PIEDRAS NEGRAS   TIKAL   HOLMUL
TONINA   LA MAR   EL CAYO   UCANLÚN   NARANJO   XUNANTUNICH
          YAXCHILÁN   YAHA   UKANAL   POMONA
          BONAMPAK   CARACOL
KUNÁ   ALTAR DE SACRIFICIOS   SEIBAL   IXKUN
CHINKULTIC   MACHAKILÁ   PUSILHA
                    CANCUEN

                    CHAMA
          NEBAJ   QUIRIGUÁ   LOS HIGOS
UTATLÁN   ZACUALPA   ACASAGUASTÁN   COPÁN
SOUTH ZONE   KAMINALJUYÚ
PALO VERDE   AMATITLÁN
EL BAÚL
JIQUISATE   PANTALEÓN
          TAZAMAL

LATE CLASSIC
(600 A.D. - 900 A.D.)

THE MAYAN CULTURE REACHED ITS PEAK IN ART, RELIGION, MATHEMATICS AND ASTRONOMY.

PRIESTS CONTROLLED THE MATERIAL AND SPIRITUAL LIFE OF THE MAYAN PEOPLE.

GREAT CITIES FLOURISHED LIKE YAXCHILAN, BONAMPAK, COPAN AND PALENQUE, BUT NO CITY WAS AS POWERFUL AS TIKAL, THE BIGGEST CITY OF PRE-COLOMBIAN AMERICA.

THE MAYAN COLLAPSE

The Mayan culture was in full splendor when suddenly, towards the end of the IX century, growth stopped and the cities were abandoned and devoured by the jungle. This is what is known as "The Mayan Collapse".

...WATER

...WATER

...WATER

...COCA COLA

What happened: drought, epidemic, social rebellion? No one knows.

More than a collapse, a reorganization of the maya took place.

The culture moved from the central zone to the north zone.

POSTCLASSIC
PERIOD

EARLY POSTCLASSIC
(1000 A.D. - 1250 A.D.)

MERCHANTS, NOBLES, AND PRIESTS UNITED. BUT NOTHING GOOD CAME OUT OF THIS FRIENDSHIP, FOR THE MAYA BECAME MILITARISTIC.

I LIKED IT MORE WHEN WE WERE A TOWN OF ARTISTS.

....ME TOO

COMMERCIAL CONNECTIONS WITH THE CENTER OF MEXICO AND CENTRAL AMERICA BECAME CLOSER.

THE POPULATION CONCENTRATED IN THE NORTH, WHERE BIG CITIES, LIKE UXMAL, MAYAPAN, AND THE POWERFUL CHICHEN ITZA, EMERGED.

NEW INDIAN GROUPS ARRIVED FROM THE CENTER OF MEXICO:

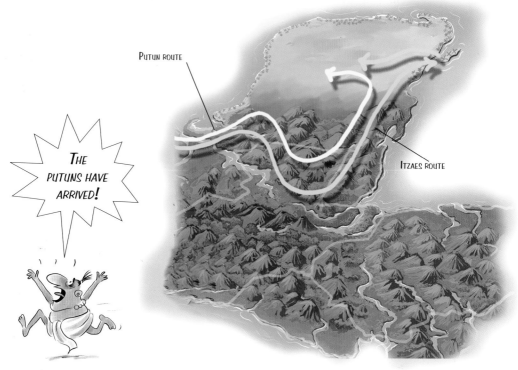

PUTUN ROUTE

ITZAES ROUTE

THE PUTUNS HAVE ARRIVED!

THE *PUTUNS* ARRIVED FIRST, COMING FROM THE SOUTH OF CAMPECHE AND FROM THE DELTA OF THE USUMACINTA, AND GRIJALVA RIVERS.

THE ITZAES HAVE ARRIVED!

LATER THE *ITZAES* ARRIVED; SAILORS WHO SETTLED ON THE ISLAND OF *COZUMEL* BEFORE ENTERING THE PENINSULA, WHERE THEY OCCUPIED SEVERAL PLACES, AMONG THEM, *CHICHEN ITZA* IN THE YEAR 918.

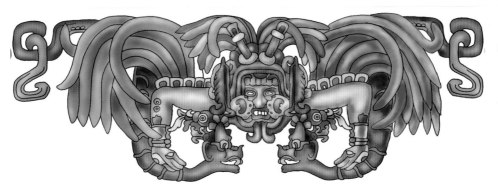

WITH THE *ITZAES*, *KUKULCAN* ARRIVED IN YUCATAN AND THE CASTLE, THE WARRIORS TEMPLE, AND THE BALL COURTS WERE CONSTRUCTED.

  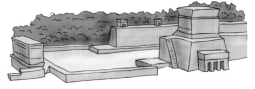

KUKULCAN FOUNDED THE CITY OF *MAYAPAN*, WHERE HE LIVED IN PEACE AND HARMONY WITH THE REST OF THE LORDS.

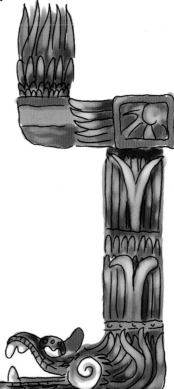

LATER THE *XIUES* ARRIVED, SETTLING IN *UXMAL*, WHERE THEY RULED FOR 200 YEARS ALONG WITH THE LORDS OF *CHICHEN* AND *MAYAPAN*.

LATE POSTCLASSIC
(1250 A.D. - 1541 A.D.)

THIS WAS WHEN THE MAYAN CULTURE DESINTEGRATED.

AT THE END OF THE POSTCLASSIC, THERE WAS A GREAT REBELLION IN YUCATAN AND THE CITY OF *MAYAPAN* WAS ERASED FROM THE MAP. THE MAYAN CULTURE BEGAN TO DECLINE.

SMALL, INDEPENDENT STATES EMERGED WHICH WERE KNOWN AS CHIEFTAINCIES.

CENPECH · CHIKINCHEL · CHAKAN · AH'KIN CHEL · TASES · AH CANUL · HOCAB · CUPUL · ECAB · SOTUTA · TUTUL XIU · COCHUAH · CANPECH · CHAMPUTON · UAYMIL

THE MAYA WERE ALREADY IN DECLINE WHEN ALL OF A SUDDEN, BEARDED AND TEMPERAMENTAL, THEY APPEARED: THE SPANIARDS FROM THE OLD WORLD.

I THINK IT'S THE OTHER HEAD THAT DRINKS THE CHOCOLATE, SIR.

THE MEETING OF THE TWO WORLDS WAS THE BEGINNING OF THE END FOR THE GREAT MAYAN EMPIRE.

BRING ME THE KING OF MAYAPAN, ALIVE!

THAT WON'T BE POSSIBLE, MY LORD:

THIS IS ALL THAT'S LEFT...

THE MAYAN SOCIAL PYRAMID

HALACH UINIC

PRIESTS

WARRIORS

MERCHANTS

PEOPLE

POLITICS AND SOCIETY

In Mayan society it was all clear: below were the ones below; on top were the ones on top and over the top.

Mayan society corresponded to the religious vision they had of the world. The priests, descendants of the gods themselves, ruled and governed.

The people obeyed and paid tribute to ensure their survival and that of their own world.

Their survival, you mean!

RULERS
THE HALACH UINIC

THE *HALACH UINIC* ("TRUE MAN"), WAS THE MAXI-
MUM AUTHRORITY OF THE MAYA. HE ESTABLISHED
THE POLITICS OF THE STATE WITH THE HELP OF THE
COUNSELOR PRIESTS AND THE MAIN CHIEFS.

GET READY: THE
LAST TIME HE WAS
LIKE THIS,

WE HAD TO BUILD
KUKULKAN'S
PYRAMID.

THE HALACH UINIC WAS THE MAXIMUM RELIGIOUS AND MILITARY AUTHORITY.

AND AS SUCH HE WAS VENERATED BY THE REST OF THE MAYA.

TO BE CLEAR: AMONGST THE MAYA, POWER WAS CONCENTRADED IN ONE INDIVIDUAL: THE *HALACH UINIC*.

PRIESTS

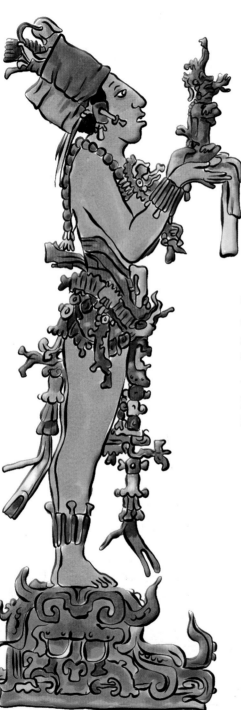

THE AHAU

THE *AHAU* WAS THE SPIRITUAL GUIDE WHO CONDUCTED CEREMONIES, WROTE THE SACRED BOOKS AND INTERPRETED THE CALENDAR.

THE *AHAU* HAD THE KEY TO KNOWLEDGE: HE KNEW ASTRONOMY, MEDICINE, WRITING, MUSIC AND THEATER.

AND IN OUR SPARE TIME WE STUDIED MATHEMATICS.

THE CHILAM AND THE AH KIN

The *Chilam* and the *Ah Kin* were the prophets who predicted the destiny of the rest of the Maya.

...AND I PREDICT A COSMIC FUTURE FOR YOU...FULL OF STARS!

THE AH MEN

The *Ah Men* was the Maya's healer. His medicine was based on divination.

HE'S A GREAT SOOTHSAYER: HE PREDICTED THAT HIS PATIENT WOULD DIE.

... IT'S ABOUT
... TIME... TO
... CALL THE NACOM...

WARRIORS

NACOM

In case of war, the control of the troops was under the supervision of the highest ranking warrior among the Maya: The *Nacom*, a guy with a short fuse in charge of war strategies.

BATAB

He was the military chief in charge of making sure people paid their tributes to the *Halach Uinic* (the *Batab*, we have to say, was almost always the *Halach Uinic's* relative).

AND HIM?

NOTHING: A TAX EVADER.

AH KULEL

The *Ah Kulel* was a sort of "town clerk," who executed the orders of the *Batab* and accompanied him everywhere.

TUPILES

They were sheriffs who executed the orders of their superiors. The *Tupiles* did the dirty work.

AH HOLPOP

He was in charge of the *Popolna*, the house where men gathered to discuss business and to learn dances for their feasts. The *Ah Holpop* was the lead singer and the one in charge of the sacred dances and the musical instruments.

33

MERCHANTS

AH POLOM

MERCHANTS AND TRADERS WERE PART OF THE NOBILITY.
AND THEY WERE KNOWN AS *AH POLOM*.

THE MERCHANTS TRANSPORTED THEIR MERCHANDISE THROUGH A NETWORK OF
ROADS WHICH JOINED THE BIG CEREMONIAL CENTERS OF THE MAYA.

THE MAYA HAD MARKETS WHERE THEY SOLD THEIR PRODUCTS. THE MARKET OF *CHICHEN ITZA* WAS FAMOUS IN ITS TIME BECAUSE *"PILGRIMS FROM EVERYWHERE CAME THERE TO TRADE..."*

EVERYTHING WAS SOLD IN THE MARKET, FROM FISH AND MEAT TO FEATHERS AND ARMS.

ALL WITH THE GOAL OF OBTAINING WHAT WAS MOST SACRED TO THE MAYA: CACAO BEANS, THE CURRENCY OF THE MAYAN WORLD.

... AND ONLY THREE EASY PAYMENTS!

THERE'S SOMETHING FUNNY ABOUT THIS CACAO: IT'S GOT "MADE IN CHINA" STAMPED ON IT.

THE PEOPLE

STAND STILL! I'M JUST A VERSE AWAY FROM FINISHING THIS POEM TITLED: "THE BURDEN OF LIFE".

AH CHEMBAL

The *Ah Chembal* (inferior men), were the ones to farm the land, erect buildings and perform all of the necessary chores so that the rest of the Maya could survive. Thanks to these "inferior men", the nobles were able to dedicate themselves to art and science.

PPENTACOOB

The *Ppentacoob's* were at the lowest of Maya society. They were slaves, prisoners of war and delinquents whom the Maya reserved as offerings for the gods.

And be thankful that we've reserved you for the gods!

MAYAN RELIGION

THE MAYA WERE PO-
LYTHEISTIC: THEY EVEN
HAD GODS FOR GOING
TO THE BATHROOM!

IN THE BEGINNING, RELIGION WAS VERY SIMPLE: NATURAL
PHENOMENA HAD TO BE INTERPRETED, THAT WAS IT.

... AND I JUST DON'T
KNOW HOW TO
INTERPRET THIS
NATURAL PHENOMENON.

In time religion became involved in every aspect of Mayan life: from art to commerce, to science, war, agriculture and architecture.

The stars and cycles of time became gods; religion became so complicated that it could only be interpreted by a few, well organized, priests.

AND IF YOU KEEP INSISTING THAT THE EARTH IS ROUND, I'LL EXPELL YOUR FROM THE TEMPLE!

RELIGIOUS FEASTS

RELIGIOUS FEASTS WERE GOVERNED BY THE CALENDAR.

THE PRIESTS WERE IN CHARGE OF CONDUCTING THE CEREMONIES.

THE MAYA LIVED IN A STATE OF PERMANENT FEAST: THEY HAD FESTIVITY ALL YEAR LONG WHICH INCLUDED EXORCISMS, SELF-IMMOLATIONS, ABSTINENCE AND FASTING.

LONG - HIC- LIVE - HIC - THE GOD CHAAC!

AT THE NEW YEAR'S FEAST, WHICH WAS HELD THE FIRST DAY OF THE MONTH POP, THE PRIESTS SUFFERED NICELY:

THEY FASTED TO DEATH AND MUTILATED THEMSELVES...THE PEOPLE HAD TO BE CONVINCED!

... AND I TOLD HIM "DON'T FAST SO MUCH CHILAM, YOU WON'T BE ABLE TO TAKE PART IN THE PROCESSION"... BUT HE DIDN'T LISTEN...

HOUSES WERE CLEANED, THE TRASH WAS THROWN OUTSIDE THE CITY AND ALL THE OLD HOUSEHOLD UTENSILS WERE DISCARDED.

SELF-IMMOLATIONS

THE MAYA BELIEVED THAT THE GODS WERE IMPERFECT, JUST LIKE HUMANS, AND THAT TO BE ABLE TO LIVE THEY HAD TO BE FED WITH OFFERINGS OF BLOOD (AND IF IT WAS PRIEST'S BLOOD, EVEN BETTER).

THE MOST COMMON SELF-IMMOLATION WAS PIERCING ONESELF IN DIFFERENT PARTS OF THE BODY.

LIKE THE TONGUE, EAR, NOSE, LOWER LIP, ARM AND LEGS...

THE SELF-IMMOLATION OF THE TONGUE WAS THE MOST PAINFUL AND THE BLOODIEST: THROUGH A HOLE IN THE TONGUE THEY INSERTED THORNED STRAWS.

...IN FACT IT'S A PUNISHMENT FOR BEING THE MOST GOSSIPY PRIEST IN TOWN...

HUMAN SACRIFICES

THE MAYA BELIEVED THAT WHEN THEY OFFERED BLOOD, THEY SENT HUMAN ENERGY TO THE GODS, AND IN EXCHANGE THEY WOULD RECEIVE DIVINE POWER.

BELIEVE IT OR NOT, THERE WERE PEOPLE WHO SACRIFICED THEMSELVES WILLINGLY...THEY WERE HIGHLY ADMIRED AMONG THE MAYA.

THERE WERE THREE TYPES OF SACRIFICES: TO BE THROWN INTO THE SACRED CENOTE, TO BE SHOT WITH ARROWS, OR THE CUTTING OUT OF THE HEART.

THEY WOULD THROW THE VICTIMS INTO THE CENOTE TO ASK FOR RAIN AND TO FIND OUT THE WILL OF THE GODS, THROUGH THE TESTIMONY OF SOME SURVIVORS. (THE WILL OF THE GODS WAS NEVER KNOWN).

IN THE SACRIFICE BY ARROWS, THE VICTIM
WOULD BE SHOT THROUGH WITH ARROWS.

IN THE CUTTING OUT OF THE HEART, THE PRIEST REMOVED THE
VICTIM'S BEATING HEART AND OFFERED IT TO THE GODS.

45

MAYAN COSMOGONY

ACCORDING TO THE POPOL VUH, THE WORLD HAD BEEN CREATED AND DES-
TROYED AT LEAST THREE TIMES BEFORE THE ACTUAL WORLD WAS MOLDED.

THE FIRST CREATION WAS A MAN OF CLAY WHO DID NOT LAST LONG.
THE SECOND CREATION WAS A MAN MADE OF WOOD WHO DID NOT KNOW HOW TO PRAISE
THE GODS. ANGRY, THEY CUT OFF HIS HEAD AND SENT A UNIVERSAL FLOOD.

THE THIRD CREATION WAS THAT OF MAN AS WE KNOW HIM:

THE MAN OF CORN.

ACCORDING TO THE *POPOL VUH* AT THE END OF THE THIRD CREATION, THE FIRST FATHER *HU NAL YE*, WAS MURDERED BY THE LORDS OF THE *XIBALBA*, WHO BURIED HIM UNDER A BALL GAME.

I STILL SAY THE GAME WAS FIXED!

HIS SONS *HUNAHPU* AND *IXBALANQUE*, TWIN SEMI-GODS, RESCUED HIM.

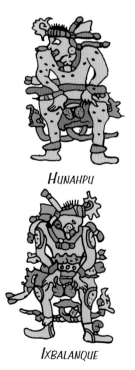

HUNAHPU

IXBALANQUE

SORRY! WRONG DOOR!

THE FIRST FATHER RESUCITATED FROM THE CRACK OF A
TURTLE'S SHELL AND CREATED OUR WORLD.

THIS CREATION TOOK PLACE ON
THE DAY 4 AHAU 8 KUMKU,

WHICH IN OUR CALENDAR IS THE
13TH OF AUGUST OF 3114 B.C.

ON THE FIRST DAY OF THE CREATION, HEAVEN WAS LYING
ON TOP OF THE EARTH AND LIGHT DID NOT EXIST.

WHEN THE FIRST FATHER ENTERED HEAVEN,
HE RAISED IT UP, AND THERE WAS LIGHT.

THEN HE ORGANIZED THE UPPER UNIVERSE: THE WORLD WE LIVE IN AND THE STARS OF THE
HEAVENS. EVERYTHING HE DID WAS WRITTEN IN THE STARS SO THAT MEN COULD READ IT.

...EENIE, MEENIE,
MINEY, MO...

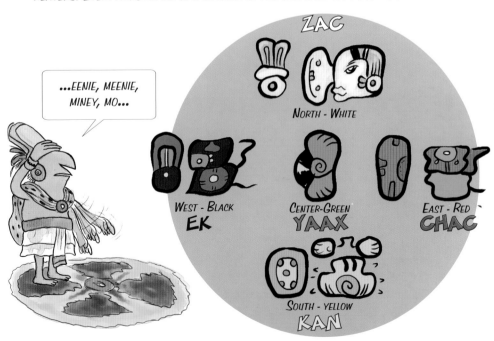

ZAC

NORTH - WHITE

WEST - BLACK
EK

CENTER-GREEN
YAAX

EAST - RED
CHAC

SOUTH - YELLOW
KAN

THE FIRST FATHER ALSO CREATED THE DIRECTIONS OF THE COSMOS
AND GAVE A COLOR TO EACH OF THE POINTS OF THE COMPASS.

MAYAN GODS

The Mayan culture was agrarian, thus their gods were related to earth, rain, and sowing. To the Maya, the supernatural energies were sacred and they were manifiested through different gods.

RUN, CHILAM! IT'S MY MOTHER-IN-LAW!

For the Maya, the gods had created the cosmos so that their own existence would be sustained by men.

Almost all the gods had a benign and generous temperament when they granted the Indian a life without anguish.
But these same gods could turn agressive: then they would unleash death, plague, war and drought.

... And that was when they were kind to us...

ITZAMNA
THE GOD OF HEAVEN

ITZAMNA WAS THE SON OF HUNAB-KU, THE CREATOR GOD OF ALL THINGS.

HE WAS THE SUPREME LORD OF HEAVEN, OF DAY AND NIGHT AND HE WAS AT THE HEAD OF THE MAYAN PANTHEON.

ITZAMNA THE PATRON OF AHAU, THE MOST IMPORTANT OF THE TWENTY MAYAN DAYS, WAS THE ONE WHO NAMED ALL THE REGIONS OF YUCATAN.

ITZAMNA IS THE GOD *QUETZALCOATL* OF THE *MEXICAS*, WHO WAS INTEGRATED INTO *MAYAN* CULTURE UNDER THE NAME OF *KUKULCAN*, THE FEATHERED SERPENT.

FIRST PLACE IN CELESTIAL BUROCRACY.

HE APPEARS IN THE CODICES AS AN ELDERLY MAN WITH SQUARED EYES AND A TOOTHLESS MOUTH, WEARING A HEADDRESS OF STYLIZED PLANTS.

ITZAMNA, THE FIRST PRIEST, WAS PATRON OF ARTS AND SCIENCE, AND THE INVENTOR OF AGRICULTURE AND WRITING.

CHAAC WAS THE GOD OF RAIN, THUNDER AND LIGHTNING.

HE WAS THE MOST VENERATED GOD OF THE MAYA.

CHAAC
THE GOD OF RAIN

WHEN THE DRY SEASON ENDED, *CHAAC'S* HELPERS CAME OUT WITH GOURDS FULL OF WATER, BAGS CONTAINING WINDS, AND DRUMS.

WHEN THEY BROKE THE GOURDS THE WATER FELL TO EARTH AS RAIN. THEY OPENED UP THE BAGS AND THE WINDS CAME OUT, WITH THE SOUND OF THE DRUMS THEY MADE THUNDER.

THE GOD CHAAC DISCOVERS A
NEW WAY TO MAKE RAIN.

THE GOD CHAAC
APPEARS ON
THE FACADES OF
BUILDINGS OF
THE YUCATAN
PENINSULA AS A
BIG STONE MASK.

IN THE CODICES, CHAAC'S EYE
APPEARS IN THE SHAPE OF A
SERPENT AND HE HAS A PENDU-
LOUS NOSE WITH A CURVED UP
VOLUTE.

AH PUCH
GOD OF DEATH

AH PUCH, "THE BARE ONE", WAS ALSO CALLED HUN AHAU, "LORD ONE", AND YUM CIMI, "LORD OF DEATH".

HE WAS ONE OF THE MOST IMPORTANT GODS OF THE MAYA.

AH PUCH LIVED IN THE DEEPEST PLACE OF THE UNDERWORLD, WHERE THE SPIRITS OF ALL THE MEN ARRIVED WHEN THEY DIED. HE IS LINKED TO THE OWL, THE CALENDAR, THE MOAN BIRD, THE DOG, AND SOME GODS, LIKE THOSE OF SACRIFICES, WAR AND CHILDBIRTH.

AH PUCH APPEARS IN THE CODICES AS A SKULL, WITH RATTLES OR EYES ON ITS HEAD, ANKLES AND WRISTS.

AH PUCH WAS ASSOCIATED WITH DEATH AND SICKNESS. ALTHOUGH HE WAS A MUCH FEARED GOD, THE MAYA SAW HIM AS A NAIVE BEING, WHO COULD BE DECEIVED WITH CLEVER TRICKS.

IXCHEL
MEDICINE GODDESS

HER NAME MEANS "THE LIGHT-SKINNED ONE", AND THIS IS WHY SHE IS CONSIDERED TO BE THE GODDESS OF THE MOON.

IXCHEL, ITZAMNA'S WIFE, WAS ASSOCIATED WITH WOMEN AND SHE WAS THE GODDESS OF MEDICINE AND PROCREATION.

... AND HE TURNED OUT TO BE DEVOTED TO THE GODDESS IXCHEL.

IXCHEL IS ASSOCIA- TED WITH THE WATER OF LAKES AND FOUN- TAINS.

SHE IS ALSO LINKED TO EARTH, THE KING VULTURE, THE MONKEY, THE SPIDER, THE DEER, WATER, AND THE WATERLILY.

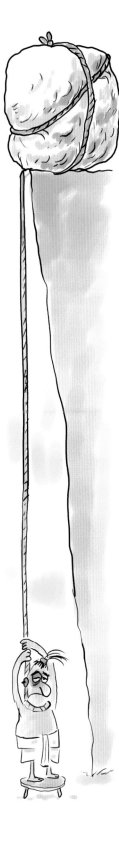

IXTAB
GODDESS OF SUICIDES

IXTAB "THE CORD ONE", WAS THE GODDESS OF PERSONS WHO HUNG THEMSELVES. TO THE MAYA, SUICIDE BY HANGING TOOK THEM TO A HEAVEN OF MILK AND HONEY, FILLED WITH PLEASURES AND DELIGHTS AND SHELTERED BY THE SHADE OF A GIANT CEIBA TREE.

YUM KAAX
GOD OF CORN

YUM KAAX WAS A YOUNG, BEAUTIFUL GOD, WHO PERSONIFIED LIFE, PROSPERITY, AND ABUNDANCE.
HE IS REPRESENTED AS A BEING IN HUMAN SHAPE WHOSE HEAD IS DERIVED FROM THE EAR OF CORN, WHICH HE WEARS AS A HEADDRESS.

YUM KAAX, "THE LORD OF FIELDS AND CROPS", IS DEPENDANT UPON THE GODS OF RAIN, BECAUSE WITHOUT THEM CORN CANNOT FLOURISH.

EK CHUAH
GOD OF MERCHANTS

Ek Chuah was the patron of cacao. The landowners honored him so that he would protect their crops.

During their trips, merchants offered incense to Ek Chuah, so that he would let them return with joy to their homes.

... And make the price of corn go up...

... Because I'm in deep, Ek Chuah!

MAYAN CALENDAR

To the Maya time was not a line which came from the past and continued to the future, but a series of connected stages continuing infinitely into the past and the future. To them time was linked to their gods and to supernatural phenomena.

For example, getting to work on time.

THE MAYA WERE THE ONLY ONES TO ELEVATE THE IDEA OF TIME AND EACH ONE OF THE PERIODS IN WHICH IT'S DIVIDED TO THE CATEGORY OF GODS.

FOR THE LAST TIME, KIN:

GIVE ME THE LOTTERY NUMBERS!

THEY REPRESENTED TIME AS GODS WHO HAD THE MISSION OF MAINTAINING ORDER IN THE UNIVERSE. THESE GODS HAD THEIR OWN COLORS AND A COURSE FIXED BY THEIR DIVINE QUALITIES.

BECAUSE WHEN I'M IN A GOOD MOOD I'M NICE BUT WHEN I'M STRESSED, I'M WICKED.

THE MAYA HAD SEVERAL CALENDARS, BUT THE MOST IMPORTANT ONES WERE:

THE TZOLKIN
A SACRED CALENDAR OF 260 DAYS.

THE HAAB
A SOLAR CALENDAR OF 365 DAYS.

THERE WAS ONE WHICH INTEGRATED BOTH:

THE CALENDAR WHEEL

THE TZOLKIN
SACRED CALENDAR

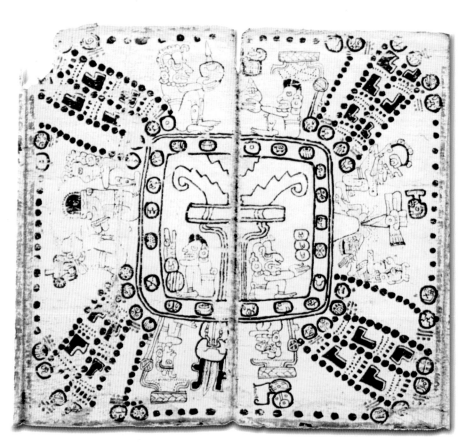

THE *TZOLKIN* WAS THE MOST IMPORTANT
CALENDAR FOR THE MAYAN PEOPLE.

*IT WAS THE SACRED
CALENDAR USED BY ALL
OF MESOAMERICA.*

WITH THIS SACRED CALENDAR THE PRIESTS CALCU-
LATED THE SOWING SEASONS AND THE BEGINNING
OF CEREMONIES.

THE PRIESTS WERE IN CHARGE OF INTERPRETING THE WILL OF THE GODS.

... AND ASK THEM TO BRING HIM AN INTERPRETER, BECAUSE HE SAYS THAT THE GOD HAS BEGUN TO SPEAK IN CHINESE...

♪ ROUND AND ROUND WE GO... ♪

THEY USED THE *TZOLKIN* AS A HOROSCOPE TO PREDICT THE FUTURE: EACH *TZOLKIN* DAY HAD ITS OWN GOD (WITH ITS GOOD AND BAD ENERGIES), WHICH DETERMINED THE FATE OF EACH PERSON.

HE'LL BE A LAZY HUSBAND!

AHAU SAYS SO.

THE SIGN OF THE DAY IN WHICH ONE WAS BORN, MARKED THE MAYA'S DESTINY: A CHILD BORN ON *AKBAL* (NIGHT), WOULD BE LUCKY, AN ORATOR AND A LIAR. THE ONES BORN ON *KAN*, WERE QUICK TO ACQUIRE DEBTS.

I'M SORRY TO SAY HE WAS BORN ON A KAN DAY.

HE HAS AN IOU SHAPED BIRTHMARK.

•••

65

IK   AKBAL   KAN   CHICCHAN   CIMI

THE *TZOLKIN* WAS THE CALENDAR THAT ALL THE MAYA USED TO KEEP TRACK OF TIME.

IT HAD 260 DAYS. THERE WERE 13 NUMBERS AND 20 DAYS WHICH WERE REPRESENTED AS HIEROGLYPHICS

HERE, THE HIEROGLYPHS

OF THE 20 DAYS OF THE TZOLKIN.

THE *TZOLKIN* WAS NOT DIVIDED IN MONTHS; IT WAS A 260 DAY CALENDAR AND IT WAS FORMED BY PUTTING THE NUMBERS FROM 1 TO 13 NEXT TO THE TWENTY MAYAN DAYS. EACH DAY HAD ITS NUMBER PLACED IN FRONT.

MANIK   LAMAT   MULUC   OC   CHUEN

EB   BEN   IX   MEN   CIB

WITH 13 NUMBERS AND 20 HIEROGLYPHS, WHEN THE COUNT REACHED 13, THE NUMBERS STARTED AT ONE (1) AGAIN, BUT WITH THE HIEROGLYPH OF THE 14ᵀᴴ DAY (SEE TABLE).

TABLE OF TZOLKIN

IK	1	8	2	9	3	10	4	11	5	12	6	13	7
AKBAL	2	9	3	10	4	11	5	12	6	13	7	1	8
KAN	3	10	4	11	5	12	6	13	7	1	8	2	9
CHICCHAN	4	11	5	12	6	13	7	1	8	2	9	3	10
CIMI	5	12	6	13	7	1	8	2	9	3	10	4	11
MANIK	6	13	7	1	8	2	9	3	10	4	11	5	12
LAMAT	7	1	8	2	9	3	10	4	11	5	12	6	13
MULUC	8	2	9	3	10	4	11	5	12	6	13	7	1
OC	9	3	10	4	11	5	12	6	13	7	1	8	2
CHUEN	10	4	11	5	12	6	13	7	1	8	2	9	3
EB	11	5	12	6	13	7	1	8	2	9	3	10	4
BEN	12	6	13	7	1	8	2	9	3	10	4	11	5
IX	13	7	1	8	2	9	3	10	4	11	5	12	6
MEN	1	8	2	9	3	10	4	11	5	12	6	13	7
CIB	2	9	3	10	4	11	5	12	6	13	7	1	8
CABAN	3	10	4	11	5	12	6	13	7	1	8	2	9
ETZNAB	4	11	5	12	6	13	7	1	8	2	9	3	10
CAUAC	5	12	6	13	7	1	8	2	9	3	10	4	11
AHAU	6	13	7	1	8	2	9	3	10	4	11	5	12
IMIX	7	1	8	2	9	3	10	4	11	5	12	6	13

THE COMBINATION OF THE 13 NUMBERS WITH THE 20 SIGNS GIVES 260 DAYS WHICH FORM THE *TZOLKIN*.

CABÁN   ETZ'NAB   CAUAC   AHAU   IMIX

POP

UO

ZIP

ZOTZ

THE HAAB
CIVIL CALENDAR

THE SOLAR CALENDAR OR *HAAB* WAS THE CLOSEST TO OUR CURRENT CALENDAR. THE MAYA CALCULATED AN ALMOST EXACT YEAR OF 365 DAYS.

THE DIFFERENCE TO THE CURRENT ONE IS OF 17 SECONDS AND 28 HUNDREDTHS OF A SECOND.

THE *HAAB* WAS FORMED BY 18 MONTHS (*UINALES*) OF 20 DAYS (*KINES*), PLUS A MONTH OF 5 EXTRA DAYS, KNOWN AS *UAYEB*.

HERE, THE HIEROGLYPHS

OF THE 19 MONTHS OF THE HAAB.

TZEC   **XUL**   **YAXKIN**   **MOL**   **CHEN**

YAX

ZAC

CEH

MAC

KANKIN

EACH *UINAL* OR MAYAN MONTH, WAS UNDER THE PROTECTION OF A PATRON GOD.

WHICH INFLUENCED EACH OF THE 20 *DAYS OF THE MONTH WITH THEIR SUPERNATURAL QUALITIES.*

20 MONTHS OF 18 DAYS GAVE 360 DAYS, LEAVING 5 DAYS OVER, WHICH WERE KNOWN AS *UAYEB* AND WERE CONSIDERED TO BE UNLUCKY DAYS. THEY WERE DAYS OF PENITENCE AND FASTING.

WITH THE FIVE UAYEB FASTING DAYS, I PAY MY DEBT AND YOU OWE ME...

(MAYA AFTER A PARTY).

MOAN   PAX   KAYAB   CUMKU   UAYEB

THE CALENDAR ROUND

AFTER THE INVENTION OF THE *TZOLKIN* AND THE *HAAB*, THE MAYA DEVELOPED A CALENDAR WHICH COMBINED THESE TWO CYCLES OF 260 AND 365 DAYS.

> THIS GREAT CYCLE IS KNOWN AS THE CALENDAR WHEEL.

4 AHAU, 8 CUMKÚ THE MAYAN DATE OF THE BEGINNING OF THE WORLD, WHICH REPEATS ITSELF EVERY 52 YEARS.

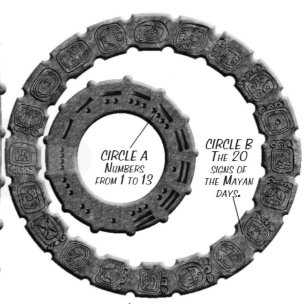

CIRCLE A NUMBERS FROM 1 TO 13

CIRCLE B THE 20 SIGNS OF THE MAYAN DAYS.

CIRCLE C SECTION OF THE *HAAB* CALENDAR, WITH THE SIGNS OF THE *CEH* MONTH WHICH IS 20 DAYS LONG.

IT'S A CYCLE OF 52 SOLAR YEARS (18.980 DAYS). IN THIS CALENDAR, EACH DAY CARRIES A "DIVINE CHARGE": ITS NUMBER AND NAME IN THE *TZOLKIN* AND ITS NUMBER AND NAME IN THE *HAAB*.

4 POP
3 POP
2 POP
1 POP
POP
4 UAYEB
3 UAYEB

4 MANIK
3 CIMI
2 CHICCHAN
1 KAN
13 AKBAL
12 IK
11 IMIX

> EACH DAY OF THE TZOLKIN, CORRESPONDS TO ONE OF THE HAAB!

THE LONG COUNT

KIN
ONE DAY

UINAL
20 DAYS

TUN
360 DAYS

KATÚN
7.200 DAYS

BAKTÚN
144.000 DAYS

TO ME, THE DAYS CAN STAY AS THEY ARE.

PENDIENTES

THE CALENDAR WHEEL WAS COMPLETE WHEN A DATE REPEATED ITSELF IN BOTH CALENDARS. BUT THIS REPETITION HAD A PROBLEM: DAYS BECAME AN ENDLESS SUCCESSION, WITH NO BEGINNING OR END.

IT WAS NECESSARY TO HAVE AN IRREVERSIBLE "TIME LINE", LIKE THE ONE WE HAVE NOWADAYS.

AND THIS IS WHY THEY INVENTED THE LONG COUNT; A CALENDAR WHICH THE MAYA EXPRESSED AS A SERIES OF FIVE COMBINED NUMBERS WITH HIEROGLYPHICS FOR LONG PERIODS OF TIME.

HE'S CALCULATING THE AGE OF METHUSELAH.

876527735892146943855,03

THE LONG COUNT STARTED TO COUNT THE DAYS FROM THE LAST CREATION OF THE WORLD.

TIKAL TOURS

AHAU 13

THE CURRENT MAYAN ERA BEGAN ON THE 11TH OF AUGUST 3114 B.C. AND IT WILL END ON THE 21ST OF DECEMBER 2012 A.D. (DAY OF THE WINTER SOLSTICE).

MAYAN ASTRONOMY

The priests spent long hours observing the sky from the summit of a pyramid.

This is how they managed to establish, with astounding precision, the cycles of the Moon, the Sun and Venus.

To predict an eclipse, the priest would announce that a monster from the sky would devour the Sun. When the Sun darkened in broad daylight, people began to panic. The priest would ask for offerings, sacrifices and submission, so that the Sun could be reborn.

... The next time you announce an eclipse,... consult the calendar properly...

... Mistakes can be fatal...

The Sun, of course, would appear again as if nothing had happened, but the Maya were left scared stiff.

Astronomy was the key to the Mayan civilization: it determined their conception of the world, their religious beliefs, and their conception of art and science.

To establish the agricultural cycles, one has to know a lot of astronomy.

The Maya were excellent astronomers.

MAYAN WRITING

WRITING WAS MADE UP OF HIEROGLYPHS WHICH WERE PLACED IN ROWS OR COLUMNS, READ FROM LEFT TO RIGHT AND FROM BOTTOM TO TOP IN PAIRS OF COLUMNS.

THE MAYAN WRITING SYSTEM WAS THE MOST DEVELOPED IN PREHISPANIC AMERICA.

THROUGH WRITING, THE MAYA ADDRESSED THEIR GODS OR RECOGNIZED THE POWER OF THE KINGS (WHO WERE LIKE GODS).

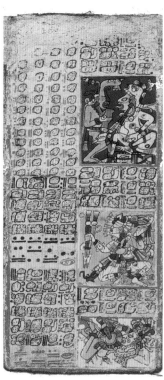
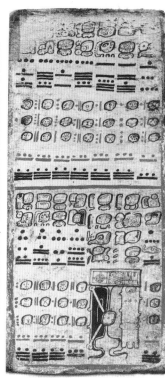

THEY HAD SACRED BOOKS KNOWN AS CODICES, WHERE THE PRIESTS REGISTERED ALL THEIR KNOWLEDGE.
ALMOST ALL THE MAYAN CODICES WERE BURNT DURING THE COLONY. ONLY THREE SURVIVED: THE DRESDEN CODEX, THE PARIS CODEX (OR PERUSIAN), AND THE MADRID CODEX (OR TROCORTESIAN).

THE MAYA WERE THE ONLY ONES WHO DEVELOPED A WRITING SYSTEM IN WHICH ANY THOUGHT COULD BE EXPRESSED THROUGH A COMBINATION OF SIGNS.

•••

MAYAN MATHEMATICS

THE MAYA PERFECTED THE MATHEMATICAL DISCOVERIES OF THEIR PREDECESSORS, THE OLMECS. THEY WERE EXCELLENT MATHEMATICIANS: WITH THEIR VIGESIMAL NUMERIC SYSTEM THEY WERE ABLE TO CALCULATE ENORMOUS FIGURES.

BUT THE GREAT MATHEMATICAL ACCOMPLISHMENT OF THE MAYA WAS TO HAVE INVENTED THE ZERO.

THE MAYA REPRESENTED ZERO AS A SEASHELL.

IT HAD ONCE CONTAINED SOMETHING, BUT NOW HELD NOTHING, ALTHOUGH IT COULD CONTAIN SOMETHING AGAIN.

THEY INVENTED IT CENTURIES BEFORE THE HINDUS, WHO MADE IT FASHIONABLE IN EUROPE WHEN THEY DEVELOPED THE DECIMAL SYSTEM.

TO REPRESENT AN AMOUNT, THE MAYA USED ONLY THREE SIGNS:

THE OVAL SHELL OR CONCH, TO REPRESENT THE ZERO.

THE DOT, TO REPRESENT THE NUMBER ONE.

THE BAR, TO REPRESENT THE NUMBER FIVE.

IN THEIR VIGESIMAL SYSTEM, A UNIT EQUALS TWENTY SMALL UNITS. THE VALUES ARE MEASURED ACCORDING TO THE POSITION THAT THE DOTS AND BARS OCCUPY FROM BOTTOM TO TOP.

7TH POSITION= 64.000.000 (3.200.000 × 20)

6TH POSITION= 3.200.000 (160.000 × 20)

5TH POSITION= 160.000 (8000 × 20)

4TH POSITION= 8.000 (400 × 20)

3TH POSITION= 400 (1 × 20 × 20)

2TH POSITION= 20 (1 × 20)

1ST POSITION= 1 (ONE)

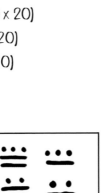

IN THE FIRST POSITION, IT IS MULTIPLIED BY ONE, IN THE SECOND BY 20; IN THE THIRD BY 400, IN THE FOURTH BY 8000 AND SO ON, ALWAYS MULTIPLYING BY 20. FOR EXAMPLE:

SECOND POSITION=20
(1 × 20 = 20)

FIRST POSITION =15
(5 + 5 + 5= 15)

35

SECOND POSITION=20
(1 × 20 = 20)

FIRST POSITION =0
(0 × 1 = 0)

20

SECOND POSITION=80
(4 × 20 = 80)

FIRST POSITION =5
(5 × 1 = 5)

85

0	11
1	12
2	13
3	14
4	15
5	16
6	17
7	18
8	19
9	20
10	

DOT AND BAR SYSTEM TO REPRESENT THE NUMBERS.

THE MAYAN ART

ART, LIKE RELIGION AND SCIENCE, WAS USED SO THAT THE RULING CLASS COULD SECURE ITS POWER.

THROUGH ART, PEOPLE REVERED THEIR GODS AND ACCEPTED THE ABSOLUTE DOMINION OF THEIR REPRESENTATIVES: THE PRIESTS.

WITHOUT A DOUBT, THEY WERE ARTISTS: ARCHITECTURE, PAINTING, AND SCULPTURE SHOW THE EXQUISITE SENSIBILITY OF THE MAYAN PEOPLE.

THE MAYA ALSO MASTERED THE MINOR ARTS AND CRAFTS LIKE WORKING WITH CERAMICS, PRECIOUS STONES, TEXTILES, FEATHERS, GOLD OR SILVER, WOOD, SHELLS, BONES, JADE, AND FLINT.

MAYAN ARCHITECTURE

THE MAYAN HOUSE

THE MAYAN HOUSE IS RAISED ON A PLATFORM; IT IS A ONE-ROOM STRUCTURE WITH ROUNDED CORNERS AND ONE CENTRAL DOOR BUILT TO FACE EAST.

THE FLOORS WERE MADE OF A WHITE PACKED SOIL CALLED *SASCAB*. THE WALLS WERE MADE OF WOODEN POLES COVERED WITH ADOBE AND THE ROOF WAS COVERED WITH PALM FRONDS OR THATCH.

THE MAYAN CITY

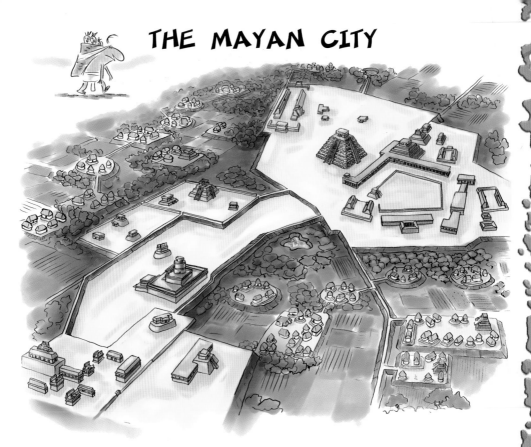

The ritual cities, with their plazas, temples, palaces and pyramids, were in reality, religious, political, and commercial centers where civil law cases were heard, war issues were dealt with, religious rites were celebrated, the ball game was played, and the market was visited.

The nobles and priests lived in palaces inside the city, obviously; the people lived close by, in their huts next to the corn fields.

MAYAN ARCHITECTURE STYLES

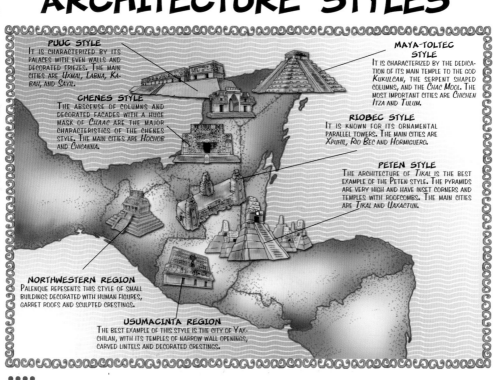

PUUC STYLE
It is characterized by its palaces with even walls and decorated friezes. The main cities are *Uxmal*, *Labna*, *Ka-bah*, and *Sayil*.

CHENES STYLE
The abscense of columns and decorated facades with a huge mask of *Chaac* are the major characteristics of the chenes style. The main cities are *Hochob* and *Chicanna*.

MAYA-TOLTEC STYLE
It is characterized by the dedication of its main temple to the god *Kukulcan*, the serpent shaped columns, and the *Chac Mool*. The most important cities are *Chichen Itza* and *Tulum*.

RIOBEC STYLE
It is known for its ornamental parallel towers. The main cities are *Xpuhil*, *Rio Bec* and *Hormiguero*.

PETEN STYLE
The architecture of *Tikal* is the best example of the Peten style. The pyramids are very high and have inset corners and temples with roofcombs. The main cities are *Tikal* and *Uaxactun*.

NORTHWESTERN REGION
Palenque repesents this style of small buildings decorated with human figures, garret roofs and sculpted crestings.

USUMACINTA REGION
The best example of this style is the city of *Yax-chilan*, with its temples of narrow wall openings, carved lintels and decorated crestings.

THE MAYAN ARCH

IT IS KNOWN AS A FALSE ARCH BECAUSE THE KEYSTONE DOES NOT ACT AS A WEDGE TO MAKE THE STRUCTURE RIGID.

THE MAYAN ARCH WAS USED TO COVER TOMBS, CHAMBERS AND ENCLOSURES. IT WAS BUILT WITH ROWS OF OVELAPPING STONES.

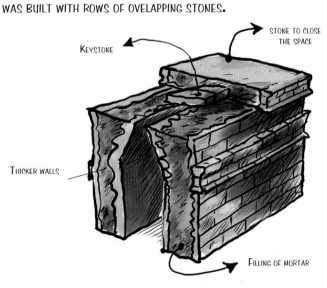

KEYSTONE

STONE TO CLOSE THE SPACE

THICKER WALLS

FILLING OF MORTAR

THE ARCH DOESN'T ALLOW FOR THE CREATION OF WIDE SPACES IN THE INTERIOR OF TEMPLES.

THE PYRAMID TEMPLE

THE TEMPLES, ON THE HIGHEST PART OF THE PYRAMIDS, WERE SACRED PLACES WHERE RITUALS WERE CELEBRATED.

ALL THE MAYAN BUILDINGS, FROM A HOUSE TO A PYRAMID, REST ON A BASE AND PEDESTAL OF STONE.

THE PYRAMIDS WERE THE FOUNDATIONS OF THE TEMPLES AND THEY SYMBOLIZED UNION.

GET TO WORK, YOU LAZY GOOD-FOR-NOTHING!

THE MAYA CONSTRUCTED THEIR TEMPLES
OVER PREEXISTING TEMPLES.

THE UPPER TEMPLE OF THE PYRAMID REMINDS US OF THE MAYAN HUT.

THE ROOFCOMB, ON TOP OF THE ROOF, GIVES THE BUILDING EXTRA HEIGHT.

PALENQUE'S ROOFCOMB

TIKAL'S ROOFCOMB

CHICHEN ITZA'S ROOFCOMB

NO, HE DIDN'T COMMIT SUICIDE: HE SLIPPED WHEN HE WAS CLEANING THE ROOFCOMB.

••••

MAYAN SCULPTURE

Most of the sculptures represent gods or Mayan leaders.

Mayan sculpture reflects the religious and civic nature of the governing minority.

In mayan sculpture we can see who was head cook in the kitchen.

TYPES OF MAYAN SCULPTURE

BAS-RELIEFS

They were part of the architectonic ornamentation, like the masks of *Chaac*, the sculptures built into facades and the pillars used as columns.

STELES, ALTARS, AND TABLETS

Were real documents in stone in which the history of great personalities was narrated.

BULK SCULPTURE

Without any direct relation to architecture, like censers, urns and Jaina statues, which represented men of different social positions.

MAYAN LITERATURE

LITERATURE (LIKE EVERYTHING IN MAYAN LIFE) WAS AT THE SERVICE OF RELIGION.
WRITING WAS SACRED, THUS ONLY THE PRIESTS KNEW IT.

THE MOST IMPORTANT MAYAN WRITING IS OF COLONIAL ORIGIN; AT THAT
TIME, WHEN THE NOBLE MAYA LEARNED THE LATIN ALPHABET, THEY
WROTE BOOKS TO PRESERVE THEIR MYTHS, ORAL TRADITIONS AND THE
MAIN EVENTS OF THE MOMENT.

BOOKS WERE SACRED AND VENERATED.

THERE'S A LOT TO BE LEARNED FROM THE MAYA.

THE SACRED BOOKS WERE KEPT AND PASSED DOWN FROM GENERATION TO GENERATION, UNTIL SOME OF THEM WERE FOUND IN THE XVI CENTURY.

THESE TEXTS WERE RELIGIOUS,

LIKE THE POPOL VUH, THE ANNALS OF THE CAKCHIQUELES AND THE BOOK OF THE CHILAM BALAM.

POLITICAL,

LIKE THE RABINAL ACHI.

OF SPELLS AND RECIPES,

LIKE THE BOOK OF THE BACAB.

AND OF SONGS AND POEMS

LIKE THE SONGS OF DZITBALCHE.

"WHILE SINGING I WILL PLAY THE HARMONIOUS, SONOROUS INSTRUMENT. YOU, FASCINATED BY THE FLOWERS, DANCE AND PRAISE GOD ALMIGHTY. LET US ENJOY THIS BRIEF BLISS, BECAUSE LIFE IS JUST ONE FLEETING MOMENT."

MAYAN CERAMICS

The Maya made all types of ceramics: from plates for food to vases to contain offerings to their dead.

In the Preclassic, decoration was reduced to stamps, incisions and simple geometrical decorations of one color.

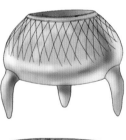

THE SPLENDOR OF MAYAN CERAMIC CAME IN THE CLASSIC PERIOD, WITH EXQUISITE CERAMICS, DECORATED WITH PAINTINGS WHICH REFLECT THE CUSTOMS AND TRADITIONS OF THE ANCIENT MAYA.

THAT'S WHY THEY ARE VERY VALUABLE FOR MAYANISTS.

...AND WHEN THE KING SAW HIS PORTRAIT IN ABSTRACT ART, HE SENT HIM TO BE SACRIFICED...

MODERN ART IS MISUNDERSTOOD.

REY PACAL

MAYAN PAINTING

IT IS BELIEVED THAT MAYAN MURAL PAINTERS WERE A SELECT GROUP OF ARTISTS WHO KNEW WRITING AND THE MAYAN CONCEPTION OF THE WORLD.

THE MURALS, WITH THEIR SCENES OF WAR AND CEREMONIES ARE AN ESSENTIAL SOURCE OF INFORMATION ABOUT THE RITES, COSTUMES AND CUSTOMS OF THE MAYAN NOBILITY.

THE MURALS WERE PAINTED WITH THE FRESCO TECHNIQUE, USING COLORS OF MINERAL AND VEGETABLE ORIGIN, AMONG WHICH THE NOTORIOUS "MAYAN BLUE" STANDS OUT BECAUSE OF ITS BRIGHTNESS.

THE BEST KNOWN MURALS ARE FOUND IN *UAXACTUN*, *MULCHIC*, *CHICHEN ITZA*, *TULUM* AND IN *BONAMPAK*, WHERE WE FIND THE MOST REFINED AND OF BEST QUALITY.

A SMALL TEASER.

MAYAN MUSIC

The music of the Maya was pentaphonic (of five tones), like that used by ancient peoples.

It had more rhythm than harmony and it was linked to songs and dance.

I DON'T THINK THAT DANCE IS EXACTLY WHAT YOU'D CALL RELIGIOUS...

THEY HAD WIND INSTRUMENTS LIKE TRUMPETS, SEA SHELLS, OCARINAS AND WHISTLES, AS WELL AS SLEIGH BELLS AND RATTLES.

FOR THE BEAT THEY HAD THE *ZACATLAN*, A BIG DRUM MADE FROM A HOLLOWED TRUNK WITH A SINGLE OPENING.

AS THE BASS DRUM THEY HAD THE TUNKUL; ITS SOUND COULD BE HEARD FROM A GREAT DISTANCE. THEY USED A TURTLE SHELL WHICH THEY STRUCK WITH DEER ANTLERS.

AGRICULTURE

THE SOWING OF MAIZE WAS AN ALMOST RELIGIOUS ACTIVITY. THE SOWING METHOD WAS PRIMITIVE. THE CROPS DEPENDED UPON THE GOD OF RAIN (CHAAC, TO BE PRECISE).

THE SOWING OF MAIZE BEGAN WITH THE FELLING OF TREES, IN THE MONTHS OF DECEMBER AND JANUARY.

HE'S AN ECOLOGIST: HE COULDN'T COPE WITH THE DEFORESTATION.

TOWARDS THE END OF MARCH OR BEGINNING OF APRIL, WHEN WHAT HAD BEEN CUT WAS DRY, THE FIELD WAS BURNT: IT WAS THE FAMOUS "BURNING".

WITH THE RAINS OF MAY, THE SEEDS WERE PLANTED MAKING BIG HOLES WITH A STICK CALLED *XUL*, WHERE THE GRAINS OF CORN MIXED WITH SEEDS OF BEANS AND SQUASH WERE DEPOSITED. LATER ALL THE SOWN CORN WAS HARVESTED.

THEY ALSO SOWED BLACK BEANS, CHILE PEPPERS, CHAYA, TOMATOES, SWEET POTATO, JICAMA, TOBACCO, COTTON, CACAO BEANS AND SISAL.

THE GODS SAY BEWARE OF AVOCADOES.

SQUASH AND YUCA. AND FRUIT TREES LIKE AVOCADO, ANONA, PLUM, PAPAYA, NANCE, SAPODILLA AND SARAMUYO.

PRODUCTION

One of the most important sources of income for the Maya was salt, which was used for internal consumption and for export.

Salt was vital in the Mayan economy; they used it as a tonic;

GET READY, WOMAN, I'VE JUST EATEN SIX POUNDS OF SALT.

And it even served to pay tributes.

AND I SWEAR THIS IS WHAT WAS LEFT OF THE CROP.

THE MAYA ESTABLISHED A REAL MONOPOLY ON SALT. THE LORDS OF SALT HAD SALE PORTS THOUGHOUT THE PENINSULA.

THE MAYA MADE PAPER OUT OF THE BARK OF THE COPO TREE.

FROM THE LATEX OF THE SAPODILLA THEY EXTRACTED GUM AND FROM THE *POOM,* AROMATIC RESINS LIKE COPAL.

THEY PRODUCED FABRICS FROM COTTON, THE CEIBA TREE, THE POCHOTE AND SISAL.

THEY PRODUCED HONEY IN INDUSTRIAL QUANTITIES, BECAUSE THE MAYA WERE EXPERIENCED BEEKEEPERS.

COMMERCE

COMMERCE WAS ONE OF THE FAVORITE ACTIVITIES OF THE MAYA, "*THE TRADE WHICH DELIGHTED THEM MOST WAS COMMERCE*", WROTE BISHOP DIEGO DE LANDA.

THEY WERE THE ONLY ONES WHO COMMERCED BY SEA AND LAND. THEY TRAVELED WITH THEIR MERCHANDISE TO DISTANT PLACES IN MEXICO AND CENTRAL AMERICA.

Maritime commerce covered all of the Yucatan Peninsula, from Tabasco to Honduras. The rivers Usumacinta, Grijalva, Candelaria, and Motagua, Motan, and Belize and their affluents, served to transport products between the highlands and the lowlands.

Yucatan exported salt, honey, wax, fish, cotton, and sisal. Guatemala exported wood, fur, cotton, quetzal feathers, copal and jade.

From the coasts of the Gulf and the Pacific came cacao beans and rubber. From Chiapas, furs, indigo, vanilla and amber. From Honduras, cacao and alabaster.

From Mexico, Oaxaca, and Central America they imported jade objects, obsidian, gold, copper and ceramics.

From the highlands and the Gulf Coast, slaves were imported.

In the regions of Yucatan, the roads or *sacbes* were used by merchants to transport their products. The bearers were known as *Tamemes*.

FOOD

THE MAYA EVEN HAD MAIZE SOUP. THEY ATE IT FOR BREAKFAST, LUNCH AND DINNER.

AT SUNRISE, THE MAYA DRANK CORN DISSOLVED IN HOT WATER; AT LUNCH IN THE CROPFIELD, THEY DRANK CORN POZOLE, AND BACK AT HOME THEY ATE THE ONLY MEAL OF THE DAY: BEANS AND SQUASH PUREE WITH CORN *TORTILLAS*.

WE'RE GOING TO HAVE TO CHANGE THE MENU: YOUR HEAD IS STARTING TO LOOK LIKE AN EAR OF CORN.

CORN WAS COMPLEMENTED WITH FISH OR THE MEAT OF OTHER ANIMALS SUCH AS TURKEY, TURTLEDOVE, PIGEON, AND DUCK; AND THE ANIMALS THAT THEY HUNTED LIKE PHEASANT, RABBIT, WILD BOAR, ARMADILLO AND OF COURSE, DEER.

... I THINK WE'VE MADE A TERRIBLE MISTAKE.

HUNTING WAS A VERY WELL ORGANIZED ACTIVITY: WHOEVER HUNTED A DEER COULD KEEP WHAT HE LIKED MOST; THE REST HE LEFT FOR HIS HUNTING COMPANIONS.

A PART OF WHAT WAS HUNTED WAS GIVEN AS TRIBUTE.

WHEN THE HUNT WAS GOOD, THE MAYA SMEARED THEIR IDOLS WITH BLOOD; IF IT WAS BAD THEY WHIPPED THEM.

...AND NOT EVEN A LITTLE DEER: YOU'LL SEE!

...LONG ¡HIC! - LIVE THE GOD ¡HIC! - CHAAC...

HONEY WAS ALSO MUCH USED; IT WAS SPECIALLY USED TO PREPARE A FERMENTED LIQUOR WHICH WAS DRUNK IN ALL THE RITUALS: *BALCHE*.

LAWS

DISPUTES, JUDGMENTS AND CONTRACTS WERE ORAL AND
WITNESSES, JUDGES AND LITIGANTS WERE A PART OF THEM.

MAYAN LAWS AND RIGHTS
WERE BASED ON CUSTOMS
AND PRECEDENTS.

THE MAYA DIFFERENTIATED FELONIES COMMITED WITH PREMEDITATION
FROM FELONIES WHICH DIDN'T HAVE A MOTIVE.

I KNOW I STABBED HIM 17
TIMES, YOUR HONOR, BUT
I DIDN'T MEAN IT.

PRISON DID NOT EXIST; THE GUILTY WERE SENTENCED TO DEATH OR FORCED LABOR. SLAVERY WAS A LEGAL SANCTION.

PUNISHMENT WAS BASED ON VENGEANCE, NOT ON THE PROTECTION OF SOCIETY.
ADULTERY, TREASON, RAPE, AND HOMICIDE WERE, FOR SURE, GIVEN THE DEATH PENALTY.

> THEY WOULD PUT THE GUILTY PERSON IN THE HANDS OF THE OFFENDED, EVEN IN CASES OF MURDER.

THEY DID NOT INCARCERATE ANYONE FOR DEBTS (NO ONE SOLD ON CREDIT). THIEVES WERE MADE TO RETURN WHAT THEY HAD STOLEN; IF THEY DIDN'T, THEY WERE FORCED TO PAY WITH SLAVERY.
A DEGRADING PUNISHMENT WAS TO SHAVE THE DELINQUENT'S HEAD.

> ... AND HE SWEARS HE'S KING PACAL, BUT WITH THAT LOOK NO ONE BELIEVES HIM.

CUSTOMS

THE MAYA WERE VERY CLEAN: MEN AND WOMEN PAINTED, TATTOED AND PERFUMED THEMSELVES WITH FRAGANT OINTMENTS AND FLOWERS.

THEY CONSIDERED DEFORMATION OF THE SKULL TO BE BEAUTIFUL, AND ACHIEVED IT BY FLATTENING THE SKULL JUST A FEW DAYS AFTER BIRTH.

...AND I DON'T WANT ANY MORE "DICKHEAD" COMMENTS.

THE SAME APPLIED TO BEING CROSS-EYED, WHICH THEY AC-COMPLISHED BY HANGING BALLS OF RESIN IN FRONT OF THE CHILDREN'S EYES.

WE KNOW THE MAYA WAY OF DRESSING DUE TO THE RELIFS AND PAINTINGS AT THE CEREMONIAL CENTERS.

MAYAN PEOPLE WORE AN *EX*, A LOINCLOTH WHICH THEY PLACED BETWEEN THE THIGHS AND TIED AROUND THEIR WAIST. THE COMMON WOMAN WORE AN *HIPIL*.

ATTENTION: MY EX IS "EXTRALARGE".

THE GREAT LORDS WERE SUMPTUOUS: THEY WORE A VERY DECORATED *EX*, COTTON CLOAKS, JAGUAR FURS, DECORATED SANDALS, AND BIG TUFTS OF FEATHERS.

THEY WORE EARMUFFS AND NOSE RINGS, THEY FILED THEIR TEETH AND INLAID THEM WITH PRECIOUS STONES.

MAYAN NAMES

A NAME AMONGST THE MAYA HAD FOUR STAGES:

1.PAAL KABA

WAS THE GIVEN NAME, WHICH WAS, USUALLY THE NAME OF AN ANIMAL OR A PLANT. FOR EXAMPLE: **CHUY** (SPARROW HAWK) OR **KEH** (DEER). A PREFIX WAS PLACED IN FRONT OF THIS NAME: **AH**, IF IT WAS A MAN AND **IX** OR **X** IF IT WAS A WOMAN.

THEN THEY ADDED THE FATHER'S LAST NAME TO PRO-DUCE NAMES LIKE: **AH CHUY MAY** (HAWK), OR **AH KEH HUCHIM** (DEER).

2.NAAL KABA

AFTER MARRIAGE, THE *PAAL KABA* WAS REPLACED BY THE *NAAL KABA,* IN WHICH THE WORD **NA** - WHICH MEANS MOTHER- PRECEDES THE GIVEN NAME. THEN THEY ADDED THE FATHER'S LAST NAME. FOR EXAMPLE:

NA CHI COCOM
NA POOT XIU
NA CHAN CHEL

3.COCO KABA

THE *COCO KABA* WAS THE SURNAME THEY GAVE PEOPLE.

FOR EXAMPLE.
AH XOCHIL ICH
(OWL FACE)

4.PROFESSIONAL NAME

THIS WAS THE NAME OF THE TRADE WHICH A PERSON PERFORMED. FOR EXAMPLE:
CHILAM BALAM
(THE *BALAM* PROPHET)
AH KIN CHI
(THE *CHI* PRIEST)

And thus we throw the last stone of these Maya on the rocks, rocks on which the author walked barefoot and under the sun to bring you, patient and self-sacrificing reader, a brief account of what was (and still is) this millenary culture.

All there is left to say is good bye; and to do it in the way *Itzamna* dictates, we shall repeat what the slave *Ah Tzab Kumun* said to the *Nacom* on the stone of sacrifice:

"U xul in t'an la'"
(this is the end of my words)

(... and mine too).